VAN GOGH

THE GREAT ARTISTS COLLECTION

MASON CREST

Contents

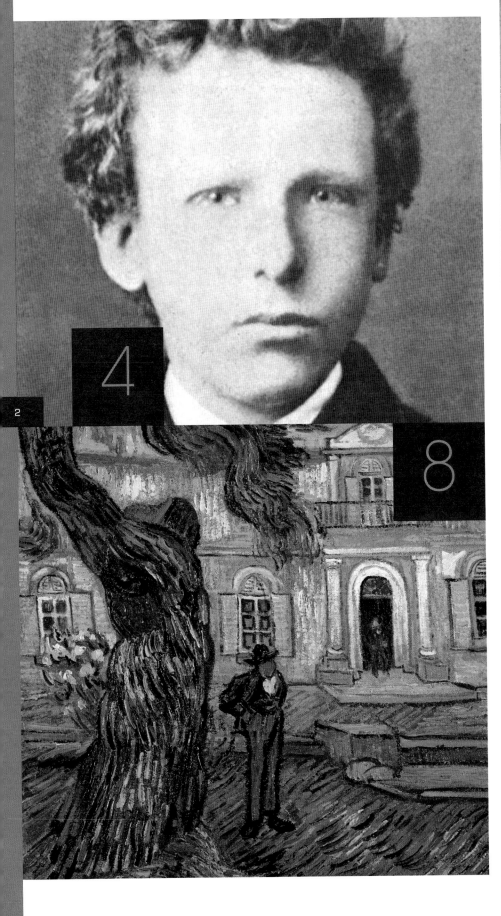

*Great Works order is alphabetical where possible.

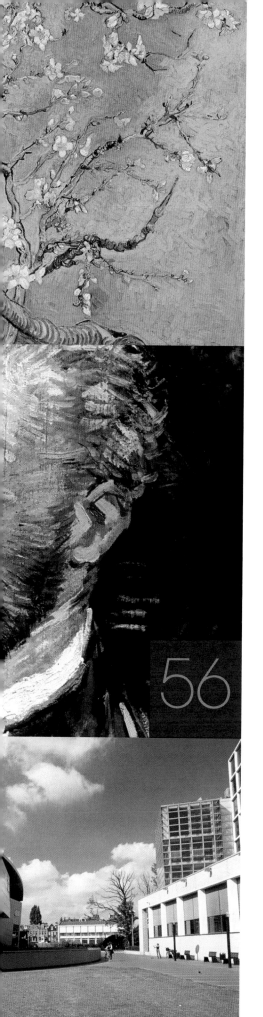

VAN GOGH

Mason Crest
450 Parkway Drive, Suite D
Broomall, PA 19008
www.masoncrest.com

©2016 by Mason Crest, an imprint of National Highlights, Inc.

Printed and bound in the United States of America.

10 9 8 7 6 5 4 3 2 1

Cataloging-in-Publication Data on file with the Library of Congress.

Series ISBN: 978-1-4222-3256-9
Hardback ISBN: 978-1-4222-3263-7
ebook ISBN: 978-1-4222-8540-4

Written by: Jessica Bailey

Images courtesy of PA Photos and Scala Archives

"*It is not the language of painters but the language of nature which one should listen to…The feeling for the things themselves, for reality, is more important than the feeling for pictures.*"

Vincent Van Gogh

Introduction

(Public Domain)

■ **ABOVE:** A young Vincent Van Gogh.

In a letter to his brother Theo in 1882, Vincent Van Gogh wrote: "There are two ways of thinking about painting, how not to do it and how to do it. How to do it – with much drawing and little color; how not to do it – with much color and little drawing." March 2013 marked the 160th anniversary of the birth of this prolific painter, who despite not receiving recognition during his 37 years, is, today, one of the world's most loved and admired artists. Van

Gogh was dedicated to his art and studied and practiced resolutely, often suffering mental and physical exhaustion, in order to hone his skills. He believed in the words he wrote to his brother and became an exquisite drawer before he developed his unmistakable style using bold color.

At the age of 28, in December 1881, Van Gogh was just beginning his life as an artist. Much of how his drawings, paintings, graphic works, and watercolors

■ **ABOVE:** A self-portrait from 1889. Musee d'Orsay, Paris.

evolved is documented in more than 800 letters, three quarters of which were addressed to Theo Van Gogh. *The Potato Eaters* (considered his first serious work), *Sunflowers* (a series of paintings which brought these native American flowers to life), *Starry Night, Blossoming Almond Tree,* and *The Bedroom* (some of Van Gogh's most recognizable and popular works) are included in this introductory book alongside other well-known drawings, watercolors, and paintings of critical acclaim.

Van Gogh produced a staggering number of works (more than 2,100) in just nine or 10 years. In his first year, he concentrated on drawing, but didn't consider that his work as an artist had really begun until he felt confident enough in his abilities to introduce color. Working day in and day out, at virtually a manic rate, Van Gogh had little or no time to fund his artistic pursuits and suffered severe financial difficulties which caused him a great deal of stress between the years of 1881 and 1890. He struggled to make a living as an artist and only sold one painting during his lifetime for 400 Swiss Francs. *The Red Vineyard* was sold in Brussels, just a few months before Van Gogh's untimely death, to a fellow artist. He was essentially driven to dedicate his time, as a Post-Impressionist painter, articulating the spirituality of man and nature, which led to a unique fusion of style. His pieces are dramatic, emotional, and have a fluid rhythmic movement, while his personal torment and mental instability show a tortured artist with a self-destructive talent whose style and methods came to define Abstract Expressionism.

Van Gogh was convinced that a great artist – a colorist – would lead the world into the 20th century. Little did he know that he was the colorist who would transform the world of art and become one of the greatest influences on modern works in to the 20th century and beyond. However, Theo Van Gogh recognized the potential in his brother's works and was confident that Vincent would eventually be acknowledged as a great artist on an international level.

(Public Domain)

■ **ABOVE:** Vincent's brother, Theo Van Gogh.

Van Gogh

A Biography

(Public Domain)

■ **ABOVE:** The Van Gogh family tree. In order: Theodorus, Anna Cornelia, Vincent, Anna Cornelia, Theo, Elisabetha, Willemina, and Pierre.

Born in Groot-Zundert, Holland, on March 30, 1853, Van Gogh was the son of Theodorus Van Gogh (1822-1885), a pastor, and Anna Cornelia Van Gogh (nee Carbentus) (1819-1907). The couple's second son, Vincent, was named after his grandfather and stillborn brother born in 1852. He was a quiet, troubled child who lacked self-confidence and was prone to emotional outbursts. Brought up in a religious household in the south of the Netherlands, Van Gogh had three sisters and two brothers. His younger brother Theo (1857-1891) was to become his life-long supporter (both emotionally and financially) and best friend. Little is really known of Van Gogh's early childhood, although the signs of mental instability were evident from a young age. As he grew older, Van Gogh embarked on two relationships that wouldn't last, and

worked fairly unsuccessfully in a bookstore and as an art salesman. His education before this had been, at best, sketchy, and he was eventually employed by The Hague Gallery at the age of 16. However, after a time in London he was transferred, by his employer, back to Paris in around 1875 where he lost all interest in becoming a professional dealer. He decided at this time to follow in his father's footsteps and devoted himself to the evangelization of the poor. He began a ministry in the mining community of Borinage, in the Hainault, a region in Belgium where he could identify with the local population. Here he developed a fascination with peasant life, which is clearly seen in many of his works. Theo, however, had other ideas for his brother's future, and Van Gogh – despite a lack of training, or, at the time, recognizable talent –

■ **ABOVE:** **A portrait by Vincent of his brother, Theo (c. 1880).**

gave in to his younger sibling's constant pressure and resigned himself to becoming an artist. Vincent severely doubted his abilities, as did his parents, but Theo Van Gogh was persistent with his belief in the aspiring artist and willingly provided the means to enable his brother to paint.

At the age of 27, Van Gogh moved back in with his parents while he tested different drawing techniques and styles. He chose a variety of subject matters, concentrating on perspective, anatomy, and shading. These early works included many aspects of peasant life and he developed a passion for drawing figures. He began lessons with Anton Mauve (a cousin by marriage) and started a relationship

(Public Domain)

■ **ABOVE:** The birthplace of Vincent Van Gogh, in the presbytery of Groot-Zundert, Holland. Vincent was born on the first floor, right window, with the flag flying below.

■ **BELOW:** Paul Gauguin was a close friend of Vincent's. Pictured is a painting of Van Gogh by Gauguin: *Van Gogh Painting Sunflowers* (1888).

(Mary Evans/Iberfoto)

(Mary Evans/Epic/Tallandier)

■ ABOVE: *Self-portrait with Bandaged Ear and Pipe*, 1889.

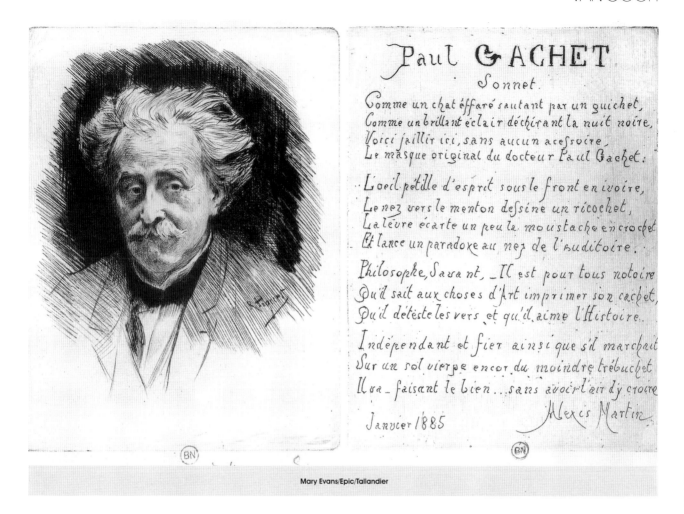

Paul GACHET
Sonnet.

Comme un chat éffaré sautant par un guichet,
Comme un brillant éclair déchirant la nuit noire,
Voici jaillir ici, sans aucun accessoire,
Le masque original du docteur Paul Gachet:

L'oeil pétille d'esprit sous le front en ivoire,
Le nez vers le menton dessine un ricochet,
La lèvre écarte un peu la moustache en crochet
Et lance un paradoxe au nez de l'auditoire.

Philosophe, Savant, _ Il est pour tous notoire
Qu'il sait aux choses d'Art imprimer son cachet,
Qu'il déteste les vers et qu'il aime l'Histoire.

Indépendant et fier ainsi que s'il marchait
Sur un sol vierge encor du moindre trébuchet
Il va _ faisant le bien... sans avoir l'air d'y croire

Janvier 1885
Alexis Martin

13

■ **ABOVE:** **Dr. Paul Gachet (1828-1909) was Van Gogh's physician during the artist's last days in Auvers-sur-Oise. This portrait was from 1885.**

with Sien Hoornik, a pregnant prostitute and mother of one, which was to lead to him falling out with his mentor who greatly disapproved of the romance, despite having introduced them. Vincent, however, continued to use Hoornik as his model, although his mood swings soon ended the affair. He then followed Mauve and other artists, such as Van Rappard, to Drenthe, a province in the Netherlands. He became enamored with the paintings of French artist, Jean-Francois Millet, who had a renowned reputation for his portrayal of peasant life, and at the age of 29, Van Gogh moved out of his parents' house to a room he rented from the Catholic Church in which he set up a makeshift studio. His fascination for the anatomical features of peasants led to *The Potato Eaters* in 1885, and while this work was to become considered one of his best early pieces, it failed to gain recognition for the artist at

the time. It was a personal failure for Van Gogh and, as a result, he enrolled at an academy in Antwerp in order to gain some professional training in art techniques.

It was while at the academy that he discovered Rubens (1577-1640) as well as Japanese art, both of which would later affect Van Gogh's style. In 1886, he moved to Paris to live with Theo where he became embroiled in the modern art of the impressionists and post-impressionists. The dark colors he'd used in *The Potato Eaters* were outdated and he quickly began to incorporate bright, bold colors, which brought life to his works. He became firm friends with Paul Gauguin (1848-1903), the French post-impressionist, (who was also not appreciated until after his death). Hoping to encourage Monet (1840-1926), Bernard (1868-1941), and Pissarro (1830-1903) to help him create an art school alongside Gauguin, Van Gogh moved to Arles in the

L'hopital Saint Paul a Saint Remy de Provence (1889). Paris, Musee d'Orsay. Peinture. Dim. 0.63 x 0.48 m. © 2013. White Images/Scala, Florence

■ **ABOVE:** *L'hopital Saint Paul a Saint Remy de Provence* (1889).

(Mary Evans/Interfoto Agentur)

■ **ABOVE:** *Le jardin de la maison des alines de Saint Remy, (the garden of Saint Paul's hospital in Saint Remy)*, **1889. This painting is housed in the Folkwang Museum, Essen.**

south of France where he was convinced that modern art required bold, outlandish color combinations. Gauguin did join Van Gogh in Arles and the two artists worked side by side, while Vincent painted sunflowers to decorate his friend's bedroom. It was these bold paintings that would help to make Van Gogh the influential artist he became. However, the artist's mental illness began to take a determined hold in 1888 and, after threatening Gauguin with a knife, the two men parted company, (following a spell of hospitalization for Vincent) although they remained in touch by letter sporadically for the remainder of Van Gogh's life. On the same day that Van Gogh attacked Gauguin, he also mutilated his own earlobe and offered it to a prostitute as a gift.

Doctors believed that the seizures the artist suffered were caused by temporal lobe epilepsy – it was believed that he had been born with a brain lesion that, combined with sustained abuse of absinthe (a highly alcoholic drink containing the toxic Thujone), brought about the epilepsy. He was prescribed the drug Digitalis, which may have caused him to see in yellow, as might Thujone, something that has been attributed to his love of color, although there are those that dispute this. Mania is also believed to have played a large part in the artist's life, from the frantic pace at which he worked to his absolute dedication. The mania was followed by depression and exhaustion and it is believed that this is what eventually led to Van Gogh's death. Manic depression (or bipolar disorder) was

(Alinari Archives, Florence / Mary Evans)

■ **ABOVE:** *Rainy landscape near Auvers,* **housed in the Pushkin Museum, Moscow (1890).**

probably the cause of this frenetic mania. The fact that the artist also used lead-based paints, which he nibbled on, or even ate in times of madness, could have also contributed to Van Gogh's complex medical conditions. Lead poisoning leads to the swelling of the retinas, which can cause circles of light to be seen by the sufferer. Many critics believe that these halo-like visions helped in the creation of paintings such as *Starry Night.* However, Van Gogh wrote continuously (as more than 800 letters testify) and it is believed he also suffered from a condition called hypergraphia (most commonly linked to mania and epilepsy) as well as suffering from sunstroke when he painted outdoors in pursuit of the realism he firmly believed in.

Although art historians, critics, and those who appreciate Van Gogh's pieces believe that many of his

greatest works came within the last two or three years of his life, it is evident that he suffered emotionally and medically during this time at a higher level than ever before. He committed himself to an asylum in Saint-Remy-de-Provence in 1888 where he found that he could not draw or paint for long periods of time, due to his mental state of mind – although *Starry Night* was created during his incarceration, as were many of his finest works. Many of the pieces he worked on during his time in the asylum contain a shaky style, which is believed by experts to be an expression of his mental state.

It is generally believed that Van Gogh shot himself on July 27, 1890, although no gun was found near his body. The artist survived for two days before dying on July 29 of his injury. Theo Van Gogh collected many of his brother's paintings from Paris, but died just six months

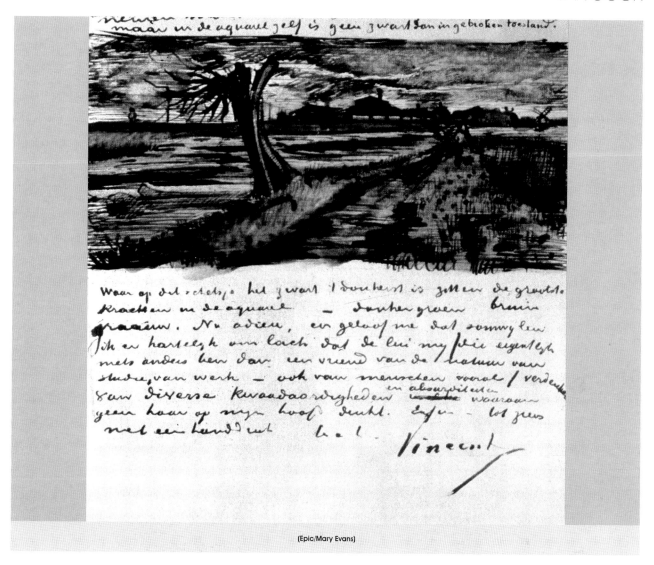

(Epic/Mary Evans)

■ **ABOVE:** A letter written by Vincent to his brother Theo in 1882, with ink and a watercolor landscape.
■ **BELOW RIGHT:** Vincent Van Gogh's gravestone.

after his older brother of dementia paralytica, a syphilitic infection of the brain. He had devoted himself, while a successful art dealer, to helping his brother maintain his artistic lifestyle and had been set on gaining the recognition for Vincent that he truly believed he deserved following his death. When Theo died, his widow, Johanna Gesina Van Gogh, dedicated herself to carrying on her late husband's quest. After publishing Van Gogh's works, Johanna brought about instant recognition and acclaim for her deceased brother-in-law. Van Gogh had believed that his life had been a terrible failure, having sold only one painting in his lifetime, however, his pieces literally turned the art world on its head, and his enduring legacy still sees him as one of the greatest artists to have had a profound effect on modern art across the globe and in to the 21st century.

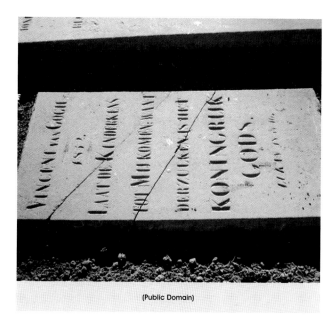

(Public Domain)

Great Works
Masterpieces

Blossoming Almond Tree
(1890)

• **Oil on canvas, 28.9 in x 36.2 in (73.5 cm x 92 cm)**

Gogh, Vincent Van (1853-1890): Branch of an Almond Tree in Blossom, 1890. Amsterdam, Van Gogh Museum. © 2013. Photo Art Resource/Scala, Florence

When Theo Van Gogh wrote to his brother to let him know that his wife, Johanna, had given birth to a boy and his name was to be Vincent, after his uncle, Van Gogh immediately set to painting a piece for his new nephew. *Blossoming Almond Tree* was part of a group of several paintings between 1888 and 1890 entitled *Almond Blossoms*. The painting was unusual at the time, both for art as a whole and the artist himself. But, these flowering trees gave the painter much joy and he painted the series in Arles and Saint-Remy to represent hope. All paintings in the group included elements of Japanese woodcut influences, Impressionism, and Divisionism, and this particular piece was created as a celebration of new life. It is well known that Van Gogh had painted almond blossoms before, but had chosen still life where cut branches were placed in a vase. Here, he has chosen to paint the blossoms against a vibrant blue sky – the painting was intended for the baby's bedroom – and it's unclear whether the painting is a still life piece where the vase and other background are obliterated by the canvas, or whether Van Gogh actually painted the branches and flowers as he saw them on the tree. However this painting was created, it shows a different style for Van Gogh and is quite unlike his other works.

Boats on the Beach of Saintes-Maries

(1888)

• **Watercolor on paper, 15.9 in x 21.9 in (40.4 cm x 55.5 cm)**

Gogh, Vincent Van (1853-1890): Boats on the Beach of Les-Saintes-Maries, 1888. St. Petersburg, Hermitage Museum. © 2013. Photo Fine Art Images/Heritage Images/Scala, Florence

Van Gogh painted a series of works entitled *Saintes-Maries* when he lived in Arles. He took the 30-mile trip to the town on the Mediterranean Sea where he created a number of pieces. *Boats on the Beach at Saintes-Maries* is described in a letter to Theo where the artist writes: "I made the drawing of the boats when I left very early in the morning, and I am now working on a painting based on it, a size 30 canvas with more sea and sky on the right. It was before the boats hastened out. I had watched them every morning, but as they leave very early, I didn't have time to paint them." The capturing of the light in the sand, sea, and sky was finished in Van Gogh's studio, and he then concentrated on *The Sea at Les Saintes-Maries-de-la-Mer* where his focus was to capture the light's effect on the ever-changing color of the sea.

Breton Women (after Emile Bernard)

(1888)

• Watercolor, 23.6 in x 29 in (60 cm x 73.7 cm)

Painting of Breton women, housed in the Galleria d'Arte Moderna of the Villa Reale, in Milan, Italy. (Alinari Archives, Florence/Mary Evans)

When Emile Bernard swapped the original painting, *Breton Women in a Meadow*, with Paul Gauguin, the work found its way to Arles and in to the hands of Van Gogh who fell in love with the subject and style of the painting. It inspired him to try the style of Cloisonnism favored by the likes of Bernard, Louis Anquetin, Paul Serusier, and Gauguin. He chose to experiment with the painting in watercolors so that he could send it to Theo Van Gogh in order to show his brother the artist with whom he was most impressed. Cloisonnism is a Post-Impressionist style, with bold and flat forms separated by dark contours.

Corridor of Saint-Paul Asylum in Saint-Remy

(1889)

• Watercolor, black chalk, and gouache on pink ingres paper, 25.6 in x 19.3 in (65.1 cm x 49.1 cm)

Gogh, Vincent Van (1853-1890): Corridor in the Asylum, September 1889. New York, Metropolitan Museum of Art. Oil color and essence over black chalk on pink laid (Ingres) paper, 1889. Bequest of Abby Aldrich Rockefeller, 1948. Inv.48.190.2. © 2013. Image copyright The Metropolitan Museum of Art/Art Resource/Scala, Florence

When Van Gogh voluntarily entered the asylum in Saint-Remy run by Dr. Theophile Peyron, he arranged for two small rooms, one in which to sleep and the other in which to set up a small studio. The rooms in this former Augustine monastery, which was converted to an asylum in the 19th century, both had bars at the windows, but from here, Van Gogh would paint a series of paintings both inside and outside the asylum walls. *Corridor of Saint-Paul Asylum in Saint-Remy*, also known as *The Corridor*, is a view down a long passage with many arches. It conjures a vision of solitude with a lone person who appears to be lost. Van Gogh's use of contrasts creates dramatic tension within the painting. The artist felt particularly alone at times during his stay at Saint-Paul, although he did gain some comfort from the fact that other patients were quite like him in terms of their own mental stability. It made him feel less isolated, however, this painting depicts a certain desperation surrounding the solitude that must have surely been prevalent at this time.

Cypresses

(1889)

• Oil on canvas, 36.8 in x 29.1 in (93.4 cm x 74 cm)

Van Gogh was both captivated and challenged by his three paintings of cypresses, which he found: "as beautiful of line and proportion as an Egyptian obelisk." This painting, completed in the summer of 1889, was one of two vertical paintings. The third is a horizontal view of cypresses with a wheat field, which was later repeated on two occasions. Van Gogh thought these trees highly majestic and the two vertical paintings, including the one shown here, comprise of "big and massive trees" at close range. When Van Gogh was well enough to venture outside to paint in late May of 1889, he began with various landscapes. This painting came shortly after in a series of paintings where he created a number of powerful scenes. This work is typical of the artist with its swirling, heavily stylized forms, and continues his developmental work and is particularly vibrant and animated.

Encampment of Gypsies with Caravans
(1888)

- Oil on canvas, 17.7 in x 20.1 in (45 cm x 51 cm)

Gogh, Vincent Van (1853-1890): Les roulottes, campement de bohemiens aux environs d' Arles. 1888. Paris, Musee d'Orsay. Peinture. Dim: 0.45 x 0.51m.
© 2013. White Images/Scala, Florence

Thick layers of impasto had become central to Van Gogh's technique by the time *Encampment of Gypsies with Caravans*, 1888, was added to his oeuvre. The idea of adding thick layers of paint – which could then be mixed on the canvas – was integral to this piece. Notice how the brush has risen off the canvas to mark the end of each stroke. Here, he was intent on the application of the pigment producing a highly expressive result. However, he needed so much paint that Theo Van Gogh had to provide more supplies. The work conveys energy and shows the transition from his naturalistic Parisian works to the vibrant colors he began to employ. It is thought that Van Gogh visited Saintes-Maries-de-la-Mer toward the end of May 1888. At that time it was still a salty plain of lagoons and marshes, and an annual site of pilgrimage for the Romany who came to worship the relics of the Marys.

Eugene Boch

(1888)

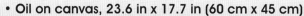

• Oil on canvas, 23.6 in x 17.7 in (60 cm x 45 cm)

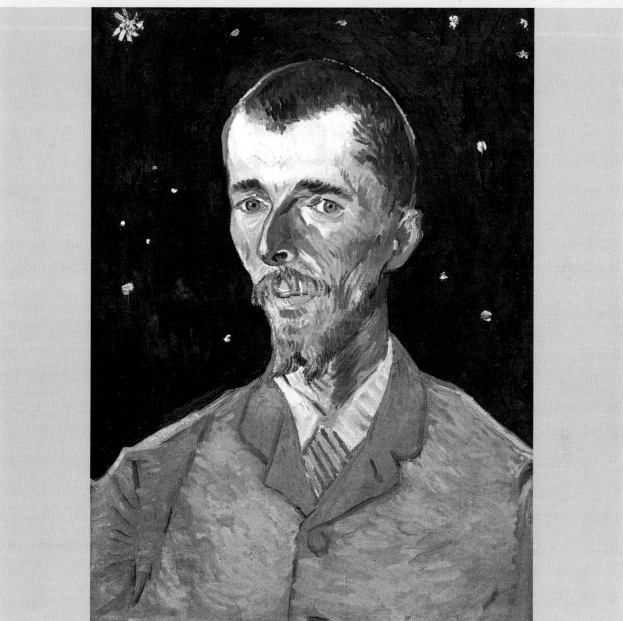

Gogh, Vincent Van (1853-1890): Portrait of the Painter Boch. Paris, Musee d'Orsay. © 2013. Photo Scala, Florence

Van Gogh and Eugene Boch met in June 1888 when the Belgian painter spent a few weeks near Arles. He was inspired to paint his contemporary with "infinity" in the background. Van Gogh said: "I will do a simple background of the richest blue, the most intense blue that I can create, and through this simple combination of the bright head against this rich, blue background, I will obtain a mysterious effect, like a star in the depths of an azure sky."

Boch sat for the artist in August 1888, and he was able to make the first sketch of the man he was desperate to paint due to his striking features and distinct appearance. Van Gogh framed the work, which he entitled *The Poet*, and it hung on the bedroom wall in the Yellow House for quite some time – it first appeared in *The Bedroom*.

Fishing Boats on the Beach at Les Saintes-Maries-de-la-Mer

(1888)

• Oil on canvas, 25.6 in x 32.1 in (65 x 81.5 cm)

Gogh, Vincent Van (1853-1890): Fishing Boats on the Beach at Saintes-Maries-de-la-Mer, 1888. Amsterdam, Stedelijk Museum. Oil on canvas, 65 x 81.5 cm.
© 2013. DeAgostini Picture Library/Scala, Florence

When Van Gogh first arrived in Saintes-Maries-de-la-Mer toward the end of May 1888, in a weeklong stay to recover from his health problems, he made two sea paintings, a village painting, and nine drawings.

This piece shows a real focus on control – there is a virtual division between land, sky, and boats. Notice too, the black contour lines around the controlled color. The small fishing village had less than a hundred homes and was the ideal place for the artist to recover from recent health problems. The light filtering across the sand, sea, and sky was finished later in Van Gogh's studio.

Head of a Skeleton with a Burning Cigarette

(1886)

• Oil on canvas, 12.6 in x 9.6 in (32 cm x 24.5 cm)

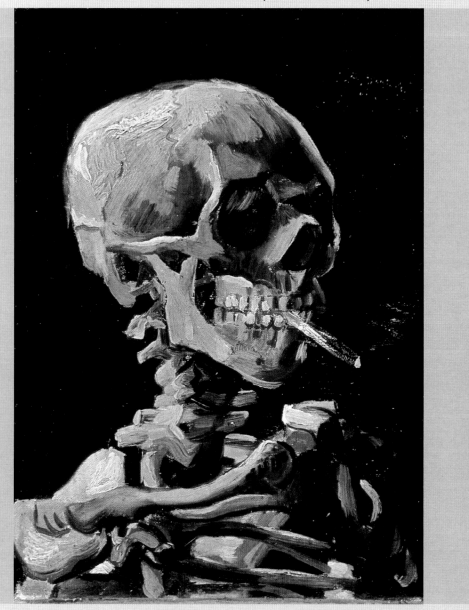

Gogh, Vincent Van (1853-1890): Skull with cigarette, 1885. Amsterdam, Van Gogh Museum. © 2013. Photo Art Resource/Scala, Florence

This unusual and interesting painting is undated, but was probably executed during the winter of 1885-86 while the artist stayed in Antwerp. He enrolled in art school – the Académie Royale des Beaux-Arts – where it was traditional to study by copying prints and plaster casts. Once students progressed they were invited to study live models, while skeletons were often introduced so that upcoming artists could understand the human anatomy – perhaps that makes this piece less macabre than it might. It is known that he attended the life classes.

Commentators cite that this painting was intended as a joke – with the burning cigarette – but that it also suggests Van Gogh's feelings on conventional conservatism within academic practices.

The burning cigarette placed between the teeth of this bare skull typifies the irreverent humor that often reigned among art students, but the striking feature of this painting is Van Gogh's vital and confident handling of a complex subject.

Houses at Auvers

(1890)

• Oil on canvas, 29.8 in x 24.4 in (75.6 cm x 61.9 cm)

This beautiful painting was created in the months prior to Van Gogh's untimely death. It depicts Auvers in the summer, showing a shaped tapestry of the landscape, in carefully crafted colors.

It is known, from letters to Theo Van Gogh, that despite the artist's impending death, he was quite optimistic and his health was far better than it had been for some time. He left the asylum in May 1890. The colors here are strong, adding to the feelings of optimism that Van Gogh experienced during his final months in Auvers-sur-Oise, a small village just 18 miles north of Paris. The artist lived at the Ravoux Inn – today, known as The House of Van Gogh – where he rented a room for 3.50 Francs a day for full board. He lodged in Room 5 in the attic rooms. The building is a French historic monument and Van Gogh's room is still in its original state. The remainder of the site was developed and renovated over the preceding years. Van Gogh may have been here a short time, but he painted more than 70 pieces while living in the heart of the village and its beautiful surrounding countryside. The Ravoux Inn was one of 37 homes occupied by the artist during his short 37 years. It is a memorial to the artist and visitors cite that the small room in the attic, where Theo watched helplessly as his brother died, is shrouded in simplicity, yet evokes powerful emotions.

Le Moulin de la Galette
(1886)

• Oil on canvas, 15 in x 18.3 in (38 cm x 46.5 cm)

Le Moulin de la Galette was the subject of a number of paintings of a windmill. It was close to Montmartre where Van Gogh shared an apartment with his brother, Theo. The windmill belongs to a sub-set series of paintings from Montmartre. The windmill – which overlooked Paris – came complete with viewing terrace, bars, cafés and a dance hall. It was built in 1622 and called Blute-Fin. It belonged to the Debray family in the 19th century. Theo Van Gogh had persuaded his brother to reside in Paris from 1886 in order to meet with Impressionists and Symbolists, among others, who might influence his work and further his development. It was here that he met Pissarro, Bernard, Signac, Toulouse-Lautrec, and Paul Gauguin. Van Gogh was not the only artist to be inspired by the Moulin de la Galette – Renoir painted a piece entitled *Bal du Moulin de la Galette.*

Lilacs

(1889)

• Oil on canvas, 28.7 in x 36.2 in (73 cm x 92 cm)

Gogh, Vincent Van (1853-1890). Lilac Bush. 1889. Post-Impressionism. Oil on canvas. Russia. St. Petersburg. State Hermitage Museum. (Mary Evans/C. Alexei/Iberfoto)

This exquisite work was completed in 1889, shortly after Van Gogh voluntarily sought treatment at the asylum of Saint-Paul-de-Mausole. The potential subjects within the asylum and its grounds offered him a number of opportunities. These included the view from his window, the unkempt gardens, and while he couldn't venture into the countryside he painted this masterpiece within the confines of the asylum. *Lilacs* was painted as his condition was assessed. The lilac bush has been composed of fragmented, separate brushstrokes and conforms to the ideals of Impressionism to a certain extent. However, it contains a spatial dynamism unknown to the movement. It is a vibrant approach to a beautiful subject, full of energy and dramatic expression. The delicate painting is also an emotional piece which, in rejecting Impressionism, shows the artist's own artistic language.

Memory of the Garden at Etten (Ladies of Arles)

(1888)

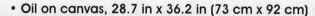

• Oil on canvas, 28.7 in x 36.2 in (73 cm x 92 cm)

Gogh, Vincent Van (1853-1890): Memory of the Garden at Etten (Ladies of Arles). St. Petersburg, Hermitage Museum. © 2013. Photo Scala, Florence

In this beautiful painting, three ladies grace the canvas against a backdrop of gardens and flowers. It was a memory of the garden at Etten that Van Gogh wished to have close by hanging it in his bedroom. The figure to the left of the piece is wearing a shawl and carrying a red parasol, while the older woman – in the middle of the piece – wears a violet shawl. The bunch of dahlias, some in customary Van Gogh yellow, stands out against the hues of blues and greens. The third figure, wearing a cap, is hunched over tending to the garden. The artist wrote on November 16, 1888 to his sister, Wilhelmina Van Gogh: "Here you are. I know this is hardly what one might call a likeness, but for me it renders the poetic character and the style of the garden as I feel it. All the same, let us suppose that the two ladies out for a walk are you and our mother; let us even suppose that there is not the least, absolutely not the least vulgar and fatuous resemblance – yet the deliberate choice of colour, the somber violet with the blotch of violent citron yellow of the dahlias, suggests Mother's personality to me.

"The figure in the Scotch plaid with orange and green checks stands out against the somber green of the cypress, which contrast is further accentuated by the red parasol – this figure gives me an impression of you like those in Dickens's novels, a vaguely representative figure.

"I don't know whether you can understand that one may make a poem only by arranging colours, in the same way that you can say comforting things in music.

"In a similar manner the bizarre lines, purposely selected and multiplied, meandering all through the picture, may fail to give the garden a vulgar resemblance, but may present it to our minds as seen in a dream, depicting its character, and at the same time stranger than it is in reality."

The painting is one of four canvases. Provence provoked memories of his hometown in Holland, and may have been inspired by his bitterness at failing to establish a Studio of the South, evoking a yearning for the past.

Portrait of Dr. Gachet

(1890)

• Graphic, etching, 7.1 in x 5.8 in (18 cm x 14.7 cm)

Gogh, Vincent Van (1853-1890): Portrait of Dr. Gachet, 1890. Budapest, Museum of Fine Arts, Budapest (Szepmueveszeti Muzeum). Etching, drypoint, 180 x 147 mm.
© 2013. The Museum of Fine Arts. Budapest/Scala, Florence

This mesmerizing etching, the only one known by Van Gogh, was completed in 1890 of Dr. Gachet, the physician who took responsibility for the artist during his darker times. Although Dr. Gachet was a medical professional, he was known to be as melancholy as his patient at times and it appears that the two men supported each other throughout their more turbulent weeks and months. The *Portrait of Dr. Gachet*, which shows a downhearted man with his pipe, was sold by Christie's to Ryoie Saito, a Japanese industrialist, for a record $130 million in 1990. The graphic was placed in storage with its new owner declaring that the piece would be destroyed on his death. Saito died six years after the etching was bought and its current whereabouts are unknown.

Prisoners Exercising (also known as *Prisoners' Round*), (after Doré)

(1890)

• Oil on canvas, 31.5 in x 25.2 in (80 cm x 64 cm)

Gogh, Vincent Van (1853-1890): Prisoners Exercising (Taking the Air in a Prison Yard). Moscow, Pushkin Museum. © 2013. Photo Scala, Florence

This painting was composed during the artist's stay at the asylum in Saint-Remy in February 1890. It was also at this time that he tried to copy Daumier's *Men Drinking* and *The Prison* by Doré. It is known through the letters that Van Gogh sent his brother Theo that he found the copies difficult to paint. He also worked on paintings after Delacroix and Millet, but the original of this particular piece was Gustav Doré's, *Newgate: The Exercise Yard*, which was included in the 1872 publication of *London a Pilgrimage*, by Blanchard Jerrold. Van Gogh was a great admirer of the late 19th-century English engravings – a time when social hardships were featured in almost every medium, from writings to art.

This is a striking piece – perhaps not for the subject matter – notice how the carefully crafted light effects in the work are stunning. There is perhaps a connection to Van Gogh's self-imposed confinement here, reflecting his own frustration and discontent.

Sorrow

(1882)

Gogh, Vincent Van (1853-1890): Sorrow, 1882. New York, Museum of Modern Art (MoMA). Transfer litograph, composition: 15 3/8 x 11 3/4 in. (39.1 x 29.9 cm); sheet 18 9/16 x 14 3/4 in. (47.1 x 37.5 cm). Purchase. Acc. n.: 332.1951. © 2013. Digital image, The Museum of Modern Art, New York/Scala, Florence

Van Gogh began experimenting in lithography in 1882 and went on to create 10 graphic works, nine lithographs, and one etching. As with his oil paintings and watercolors, the artist was successful in this medium, however, chose not to work in this way often. *Sorrow*, completed in 1882, is a lithograph of Sien Hoornik, which was originally a drawing. It was to be the most important work of his partnership with the pregnant woman who already had a five-year-old daughter. This beautiful piece was described by the artist as: "…the best figure I have drawn yet."

Starry Night
(1889)

• Oil on canvas, 29 in x 36.3 in (73.7 cm x 92.1 cm)

Gogh, Vincent van (1853-1890): The Starry Night, 1889. New York, Museum of Modern Art (MoMA). Oil on canvas, 29 x 36.3 in. (73.7 x 92.1 cm).
Acquired through the Lillie P. Bliss Bequest. Acc. n.:472.1941© 2013. Digital image, The Museum of Modern Art, New York/Scala, Florence

Starry Night, completed in 1889, is one of the artist's most popular works. In fact, since the 1940s it has been considered as perhaps his greatest achievement. It is well known that Van Gogh took solace and security from the nighttime, he considered it a time for reflection, but he was not oblivious to the darker side of night. There has been much discussion as to whether Van Gogh painted this piece due to his condition whilst in the asylum in Arles, however, through his letters to Theo it is known that he also chose to paint the stars at night in order to remain close to religion – a constant from his early childhood. The painting shows the village of Saint-Remy in a view from the asylum to the north, but the cypress tree was added to the composition. Although the swirling features may be exaggerated, note that this piece depicts a scene easily related to on every level.

Starry Night over the Rhone

(1888)

• Oil on canvas, 28.5 in x 36.2 in (72.5 cm x 92 cm)

Gogh, Vincent Van (1853-1890): Starry night. Arles, 1888. Paris, Musee d'Orsay. Oil on canvas, 72.5 x 92 cm.© 2013. Photo Scala, Florence

Alongside *Starry Night* and *The Café Terrace on the Place du Forum, Arles at Night,* this painting makes up Van Gogh's starry night paintings. Unlike its successor, *Starry Night,* this painting features people to the bottom right of the canvas. The feel of the painting is natural, although it has never gained the popularity of the other pieces. The scene is taken from the quayside on the banks of the Rhone in Lamartine, close to the Yellow House where Van Gogh rented rooms. The artist was intrigued by the challenges that painting at night posed and the reflections of the new (at the time) artificial lights – depicted here as gaslights in bold yellow. The stars, also a recognizable Van Gogh yellow, are a different shade, but no less interesting given that they are surrounded by their own orbs of light. Notice how warm the reflections and stars are against the brooding dark background.

Still Life: Vase with Fifteen Sunflowers

(1888)

- Oil on canvas, 35.9 in x 28.7 in (91.2 cm x 73 cm)

Gogh, Vincent Van (1853-1890): Sunflowers, 1888. London, National Gallery. Oil on canvas, 92.1 x 73 cm. Bought, 1924. Acc.n.: NG3863. One of four paintings of sunflowers intended to decorate Gauguin's room in the Yellow House. Van Gogh produced a replica of this painting in January 1889. © 2013. Copyright The National Gallery, London/Scala, Florence

Each of the sunflowers paintings are clearly recognizable as works of Van Gogh, and *Still Life: Vase with Fifteen Sunflowers*, completed in August 1888, is the fourth version of the group. As with the other paintings, this particular work contains some minor differences that separate it from the other pieces, although the layout, textures, and actual positions of the sunflowers mirror those to which this painting is most closely related. Created in Arles, Van Gogh wrote: "Now that I hope to live with Gauguin in a studio of our own, I want to make decorations for the studio. Nothing but big flowers." When the artist painted these pictures, there had been recent innovations in the manufacture of pigments, which led to chrome yellow. It is thought that without these developments, Van Gogh would have struggled to create the intensity of the flowers, which he so obviously managed through bold color. Note how he still keeps the vitality of life-affirming flowers in contrast with those that are dying.

Still Life: Vase with Irises

(1890)

• Oil on canvas, 29 in x 36.3 in (73.7 cm x 92.1 cm)

Van Gogh painted four still life floral pieces, which were all completed in May 1890. Now housed in the Metropolitan Museum of Art in New York City, this work, *Still Life: Vase with Irises*, shows that the red lake pigment the artist used has faded. As a result, the irises now appear blue, while Van Gogh wrote himself that: "…the effect is soft and harmonious because of the combination of greens, pinks, and violets." The background which the artist created almost appears white in the painting today. When Van Gogh arrived at the asylum in Saint-Remy he chose to paint the hospital's overgrown garden. For nearly a year, he rejected still life paintings until he created the four floral pieces: two with irises and two with roses. One vase of irises was placed against a pink background – the painting depicted here – while the other was against a citron yellow background. Van Gogh's mother owned this painting, until her death in 1907.

Still Life: Vase with Twelve Sunflowers

(1889)

• Oil on canvas, 36.4 in x 28 in (92.4 cm x 71.1 cm)

Gogh, Vincent Van (1853-1890): Sunflowers, 1888 or 1889. Philadelphia, Philadelphia Museum of Art. Oil on canvas 36 3/8 x 28 in. (92.4 x 71.1 cm). The Mr. and Mrs. Carroll S. Tyson, Jr., Collection, 1963.© 2013. Photo The Philadelphia Museum of Art/Art Resource/Scala, Florence

The series of sunflowers paintings were to have a profound effect on the art community and would influence thousands of artists the world over for generations to come. These paintings are synonymous with the artist and proved to be one of the most popular series of paintings ever created (as well as the most reproduced). This particular painting, *Still Life: Vase with Twelve Sunflowers,* is a repetition of the third version by Van Gogh, completed in 1889. Neither the original paintings (created in 1888) or their later versions contained the numbers of flowers that Van Gogh indicated in his announcement about the series. Each sunflower picture flows through the vibrancy of life with bright full blooms of yellow, to ultimately death, shown in contrast with browning, lifeless flowers. Yet, the paintings are bright, cheerful, and capture a feeling of awakening.

Thatched Cottages

(1890)

- Oil on canvas, 23.6 in x 28.7 in (60 cm x 73 cm)

Gogh, Vincent Van (1853-1890): Old Farmhouses, 1890. St. Petersburg, Hermitage Museum. 60 x 73 cm. © 2013. Photo Scala, Florence

Van Gogh spent the last few months of his life in Auvers-sur-Oise following his departure from the asylum in Saint-Remy in May 1890. It was here, in a small town just north of Paris, that he completed at least 70 paintings in the 70 days that he lived in Auvers and the final days of his life. He continued to work frenetically with complete focus and concentration. This painting, *Thatched Cottages*, was completed in the same month he left the asylum and it is believed he wrote to his brother about this painting, having not worked for a short time, stating: "Now I have a study of old thatched roofs with a field of peas in flower and some wheat in the foreground, hilly background. A study which I think you'll like." It was after this time that he began to greatly suffer from further depression and erratic behavior, and his letters to Theo became less coherent. However, within his works, Van Gogh turned his direction toward portraits and had a desire to create paintings "which would appear after a century to people living then as apparitions." He clearly managed to achieve this in portraits such as *Mademoiselle Gachet at the Piano* and *Two Children*, although his continued use of landscapes, however, showed perhaps a new desolation, in paintings such as *Wheat Field under Clouded Sky*. The landscapes that made up these final double square canvases smacked of sadness and extreme loneliness.

The Café Terrace on the Place du Forum, Arles at Night
(1888)

• Oil on canvas, 29 in x 36.3 in (73.7 cm x 92.1 cm)

Cafe-terrace at night (Place du forum in Arles), 1888. (Mary Evans Picture Library/Imagno)

Also known as *Café Terrace At Night*, this painting offers a new perspective on light and dark as well as a star-filled sky. Unlike *The Potato Eaters*, however, the light and dark in this work are fairly evenly matched with the bright floodlit yellow wall to the left and the darker side of the street to the right. In addition, the stars themselves are less obvious than those in Van Gogh's *Starry Night* and other starry night pieces. The yellow wall also draws the attention and it takes a moment to leave the brightness café explore the darker side of the street and night sky.

The Church in Auvers-sur-Oise, View from the Chevet
(1890)

• Oil on canvas, 37 in x 29.1 in (94 cm x 74 cm)

Gogh, Vincent van (1853-1890): Eglise d'Auvers sur Oise, vue du chevet. 1890. Olio su tela cm. 94 x 74. Paris, Musee d'Orsay. © 2013. A. Dagli Orti/Scala, Florence

After all the trauma of the failure of the studio he envisioned in the south of France, the stay at the asylum in Saint-Remy, and while he was regaining his health, Van Gogh chose to settle in Auvers-sur-Oise, a small village on the outskirts of Paris. While here, Theo encouraged him to see Dr. Gachet (both a painter himself and a friend of many other artists) for treatment. During this time, the artist made a number of drawings and around 70 paintings in a short two-month period. While Van Gogh included the church in a number of paintings – particularly in the background of village landscapes – this was the only full depiction he composed. The actual church was built in the 13th century in the early Gothic style. It is flanked by two Romanesque chapels. This exquisite work is particularly unlike those of the Impressionists – there is no rendering of light as Monet carefully crafted on his series of Rouen Cathedral, for example. Rather, this is more an "expression" of the church than an "impression," giving rise to the expectation of the Expressionism to come and the work of the Fauvists. Here the gray and violet colors stand out against the engaging deep blue of the sky. There is a pink glow of sunshine in the foreground giving the overall work an expressive feel.

The Dance Hall in Arles

(1888)

• Oil on canvas, 25.6 in x 31.9 in (65 cm x 81 cm)

Gogh, Vincent Van (1853-1890): Dance Hall. Paris, Musee d'Orsay. © 2013. Photo Scala, Florence

This is a vibrant, "busy" work. Created at the time that Van Gogh had persuaded Paul Gauguin to visit the south of France, it was hoped that the two artists could establish the Studio of the South. However, Gauguin was fiercely independent and objected to his contemporary's overbearing presence. They managed to work together between September and December 1888 despite their differences, but it wasn't to last. There was a violent row between the two men and Gauguin had little choice but to leave Arles. (They did write to each other after their forced separation, but they were never to meet again.)

The Dance Hall in Arles was one of two stunning pieces composed by Van Gogh while he and Gauguin worked together in the fall of 1888. The other is The Arlésiennes. Returning to this particular piece, it is thought to be a depiction of an evening at the Folies-Arlésiennes, on the Boulevard des Lices. While undoubtedly a masterpiece, it is a particularly dark work, which suggests a more sinister interpretation than might be gleaned at a first glance; that "night life" can hide a multitude of sins under the guise of respectable dancing.

The Italian Woman

(1887)

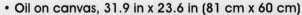

• Oil on canvas, 31.9 in x 23.6 in (81 cm x 60 cm)

Gogh, Vincent Van (1853-1890): Portrait of Agostina Segatori (The Italian Woman), 1887. Paris, Musee d'Orsay. Oil on canvas, 81 x 60 cm. © 2013. Photo Scala, Florence

This is a beautiful depiction of Agostina Segatori (1842-1910), a former model for Corot, Manet, and Gérôme. Around this time, the artist was introduced to the color theories of the Neo-Impressionists, while becoming increasingly interested in Japanese etchings. These two influences can be seen clearly in this portrait. Notice the asymmetrical border, and the fact that the figure is stylized within the portrait. There are no shadows or perspective. The background is monochrome but the work still exudes energy with juxtaposed colors to provide intensity. This work, in particular, shows such a move toward Expressionism that hints Van Gogh was a forerunner of Fauvism.

The Langlois Bridge at Arles with Women Washing
(1888)

• Oil on canvas, 21.3 in x 25.6 in (54 cm x 65 cm)

Gogh, Vincent Van (1853-1890): The bridge of Langlois, 1888. Otterlo, Kroeller-Mueller Museum. © 2013. DeAgostini Picture Library/Scala, Florence

Four oil paintings of the Langlois Bridge at Arles were created. Four drawings and one watercolor were also composed using this subject. The influence of Japanese woodcut prints is evident here in the simplified use of color, which creates a harmonious and unified work. Van Gogh's technique of using impasto – or thick layers of paint – is also clear. He uses this to apply his color so as to depict the reflection of light, which gives the painting a vibrant feel. It is suggested that the scene, including the drawbridge over the canal, reminded him of the Netherlands. The reconstructed Langlois Bridge is now named Pont Van Gogh. The work was composed at a time when Van Gogh had returned to using a reed pen for his drawings – another sign of a return to his roots.

The Old Mill

(1888)

• Oil on canvas, 25.5 in x 21.3 in (64.8 cm x 54 cm)

Gogh, Vincent Van (1853-1890): The Old Mill. 1888. Buffalo (NY), Albright-Knox Art Gallery. Oil on canvas, support: 25 1/2 x 21 1/4 in. (64.77 x 53.97 cm.); framed: 32 3/4 x 28 3/4 x 3 1/2 in. (83.185 x 73.025 x 8.89 cm). Bequest of A. Conger Goodyear, 1966.© 2013. Albright Knox Art Gallery/Art Resource, NY/Scala, Florence

The colors and light that Van Gogh found in Arles provided him with much inspiration when he moved there in February 1888. *The Old Mill* was one of more than 200 paintings that he created within 15 months of moving there. Here, his joy at being in sunnier climes and the inspiration of the colors are shown through the beauty, light, and warmth in the piece. The brushstrokes are carefully applied; short directional ones are used for the foliage. Long, vertical brushstrokes are used for the fence posts, and smooth curved strokes are used for the sky. Van Gogh was sometimes criticized for working too quickly, but this shows the thought and care taken with the work.

The Olive Orchard

(1889)

• Oil on canvas, 28.6 cm x 36 in (72.7 cm x 91.4 cm)

Gogh, Vincent Van (1853-1890): Women Picking Olives, 1889-90. New York, Metropolitan Museum of Art. Oil on canvas, 28 5/8 x 36 in. (72.7 x 91.4 cm).
The Walter H. and Leonore Annenberg Collection, Gift of Walter H. and Leonore Annenberg, 1995, Bequest of Walter H. Annenberg, 2002. Acc.n.: 1995.535
© 2013. Image copyright The Metropolitan Museum of Art/Art Resource/Scala, Florence

Toward the latter half of 1889, Van Gogh created around 15 paintings of olive trees. The subject, however, was not an easy one for him. He wrote to Theo: "They are old silver, sometimes with more blue in them, sometimes greenish, bronzed, fading white above a soil which is yellow, pink, violet tinted orange... very difficult." It is cited that Van Gogh found olive groves beautiful and old with a touch of secrecy about the "rustle," of the trees.

The Potato Eaters
(1885)

Gogh, Vincent Van (1853-1890). The Potato Eaters. Post-Impressionism. Oil on canvas. (Mary Evans/Iberfoto)

This painting was Van Gogh's first ambitious attempt, which he hoped would cement his reputation as an artist amongst his peers on an international playing field. However, the dark nature of the picture was considered totally out-of-date, and Van Gogh was bitterly disappointed by its failure to bring him the recognition he craved. It was deliberately painted to challenge its creator to the maximum of his artistic abilities at the time. He wanted to be a "true peasant painter," and this piece shows his considerable dedication to painting figures honestly with emotion but without sentimentality. Completed in 1885, *The Potato Eaters* is now considered by many to be one of Van Gogh's earliest acclaimed achievements. Note the challenges this painting renders in its contrasts between light and dark.

The Red Vineyard

(1888)

• Oil on canvas, 29.5 in x 36.6 in (75 cm x 93 cm)

The Red Vineyard of Arles, housed in the Pushkin Museum, Moscow. (Alinari Archives, Florence/Mary Evans)

49

The Red Vineyard sold to Anna Boch, an impressionist painter, at the Annual Exhibition of Les XX in 1890 in Belgium, for 400 Swiss Francs, just a few months before Van Gogh's death. It is reputed to be the only painting that he sold during his lifetime. Boch was an art collector as well as a painter herself, while her brother Eugene Boch, another impressionist painter, was a friend of Van Gogh's. The picture is striking, with its harvesters working against the sunset. It was a painting that the artist would paint from memory and the bold colors immediately stand out. It should not be forgotten that Van Gogh was pushing against the world of academic painting with his cleverly juxtaposed colors. It may have been fairly scandalous in its day, but it is this bold and frank braveness that set the scene for modern art, despite the fact that academics and critics of the time failed to recognize the aesthetic value of Van Gogh's works. Modern critics believe that this striking example of his work was literally groundbreaking. The intensity of the artist's creations is stated, by many, as "genius." This painting was acquired by Russian art collector Sergei Shchukin before being nationalized.

The Restaurant de la Sirene

(1887)

• Oil on canvas, 22.4 in x 26.8 in (57 cm x 68 cm)

Gogh, Vincent Van (1853-1890): Restaurant de la Sirene, 1887. Paris, Musee d'Orsay. Oil on canvas, 57 x 68 cm. © 2013. Photo Scala, Florence

It would have been usual for Van Gogh to take even a modest holiday during the summer months, so he therefore found subjects close to where he lived. While living in Paris with Theo, he found the town of Asnières, on the banks of the Seine, not far from the city. Here he painted and drew a number of views and landscapes, including this one of the Restaurant de la Sirene. This is possibly one of the artist's closest works in the Impressionist style, but even the parallel hatching suggests a personal style that had yet to reach its peak.

The Siesta (after Millet)

(1889-1890)

• Oil on canvas, 28.7 in x 35.8 in (73 cm x 91 cm)

Gogh, Vincent Van (1853-1890): The Siesta. Paris, Musee d'Orsay. © 2013. Photo Scala, Florence

This beautiful depiction is after Millet's *Four Moments in the Day*. Van Gogh copied a number of Millet's works, who he considered to be a highly modern painter; however, he still makes the piece his own – despite his faithfulness to the original – by the use of contrasting complementary colors including blue-violet and yellow-orange and his characteristic intensity.

The Zouave

(1888)

• Watercolor, reed pen and ink, wax crayon, 12.4 in x 9.3 in (31.5 cm x 23.6 cm)

Gogh, Vincent Van (1853-1890): The Zouave, c. June 20, 1888. New York, Metropolitan Museum of Art. Reed pen and brown ink, wax crayon, and watercolor, over graphite, wove paper, 12 3/8 x 9 5/16 in. (31.5 x 23.6 cm). Gift of Emanie Philips, 1962. Acc.n.: 62.151. © 2013. Image copyright The Metropolitan Museum of Art/Art Resource/Scala, Florence

This was Van Gogh's first real attempt at portraiture in Arles. The work served as a color study for the bust-length portrait of a young soldier. He sent this watercolor, with dedicatory inscription, to his friend, Emile Bernard. It is of a young Zouave and the first in a series of character portraits he completed while in the south of France.

Torn Up Street with Diggers

(1882)

- **Drawing, pencil, ink, watercolor on paper, 16.9 in x 24.8 in (43 cm x 63 cm)**

Gogh, Vincent Van (1853-1890): Street Workers. Berlin, Kupferstichkabinett, Staatliche Museen zu Berlin. Pen, China ink, pencils, and pastel, 43 x 62.8 cm.
Inv.: SZ 5. Photo: Joerg P. Anders.© 2013. Photo Scala, Florence/BPK, Bildagentur fuer Kunst, Kultur und Geschichte, Berlin

This drawing, heightened with white and colors, is related to the piece *Men Digging* and was created around the same time as the lost version of *Sorrow*. The work clearly shows the bakery in the Noordstraat in The Hague to the right. This indicates that the view is depicted from Sien's mother's house next door to the South Holland Brewery. In a letter to brother Theo in April 1882, Van Gogh wrote: "I fear that the better I draw, the more trouble and opposition I'll encounter. Because I'll have to suffer greatly for various idiosyncrasies that I cannot change. First of all, my appearance and manner of speaking and clothing, and also because later, when I'm earning more, I'll continue to live in a different sphere from most other painters, because of my view of things, the subjects I want to depict, inevitably demand it. Enclosed is a little sketch of Diggers. I'll tell you why I'm enclosing it… it was made in the Geest district in the drizzle, standing in a street in the mud, in all that bustle and noise, and I'm sending it to show you that my sketchbook proves that I try to capture things first-hand."

Vincent's Bedroom in Arles

(1888)

• Oil on canvas, 28.3 in x 35.4 in (72 cm x 90 cm)

Van Gogh's bedroom in Arles (1889). (Mary Evans Picture Library/Imagno)

It seems that Van Gogh was quite taken with the painting of his bedroom, completed in October 1888. Despite the fact that this painting has a left-hand corner, the bedroom at 2 Place Lamartine in Arles, was actually trapezoid with an obtuse angle to the left and an acute angle to the right because the modest property was situated on a corner of the street. This doesn't seem to have worried the artist who shows clearly that there was a "corner." Having arrived in Arles, Van Gogh had soon found hotel accommodation expensive and he moved to Place Lamartine – known as the Yellow House – where he hoped to set up his studio with Gauguin. The door to the left of the room in this painting shows where Van Gogh's friend and fellow artist slept when he did join him in Arles. There were three similar paintings of Van Gogh's bedroom and the group is referred to as *Bedroom in Arles*, or *The Bedroom*. Interestingly, Van Gogh doesn't include shadows in the picture, which follows the style of Japanese prints that the artist had studied intently. As a result, the lack of shadows and distortion of the room give the painting a slightly unusual perspective where some of the items within the room appear to be toppling over. This painting appears to give hope for the future, despite its unusual style.

Vincent's Chair with his Pipe

(1888)

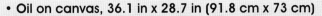

• Oil on canvas, 36.1 in x 28.7 in (91.8 cm x 73 cm)

Gogh, Vincent Van (1853-1890): Van Gogh's Chair, 1888. London, National Gallery. Oil on canvas, 91.8 x 73 cm. Bought, 1924. Acc.n.: 1807. © 2013.
Copyright The National Gallery, London/Scala, Florence

Interestingly, this painting, *Vincent's Chair with his Pipe*, along with another piece, *Gauguin's Chair*, is among the most analyzed of Van Gogh's works. The reason for this appears to be symbolism which is clear when the painting here – with its light wood – is contrasted to that of Gauguin's which is extremely dark by comparison. The two paintings side by side make for intriguing subject matter and interpretations. It has been noted by experts that should the two paintings be exhibited together, then often Gauguin's chair is placed to the left with Van Gogh's to the right, therefore facing away from each other. Interpretation of this has culminated in referencing the difficult relationship that the two friends sometimes endured. However, if you place Van Gogh's chair to the left and Gauguin's to the right, the reverse is true, perhaps symbolizing friendship and mutual respect rather than disdain and a turbulent relationship. Although Van Gogh wrote often about the paintings in his letters, he never fully explained the underlying interpretations that the pieces represented. Van Gogh's chair is plain and simple on a plain tiled floor – perhaps a representation of how he saw himself compared to his friend – who is represented by a much more ornate and sophisticated chair. However, experts disagree whether the explanation, interpretation, and symbolism is this simple. There are those that express the opinion that Van Gogh had an extreme hatred of his mother – although there is no evidence to support this – and a blatant desire for a sexual relationship with Gauguin, despite lack of evidence for this also. It seems far more likely that the chairs are just that, chairs, and that the symbolism – or not – may be interpreted in a variety of ways.

Great Works

Self-portraits

Self-portrait

(1887)

• Oil on canvas, 18.5 in x 13.8 in (47 cm x 35 cm)

A Self-portrait, 1887, oil on canvas. Musee d'Orsay, Paris, France. (Mary Evans/Interfoto Agentur)

The earliest surviving self-portrait of Van Gogh is dated 1886. This self-portrait pictured was one of 30 painted by the artist between 1886 and 1889 which places him as one of the most prolific self-portraitists of all time. The reason for this was in pursuit of the development of his art. Money for models was scarce, and as well as developing his talents as a landscape artist, Van Gogh was determined to capture the essence of figures. Using himself as a model allowed him to experiment with his style without the need for expense. He used a mirror in order to paint himself so, in reality, the right side of the face is actually the left side. His self-portrait, *Self-portrait without Beard*, was the last portrait he painted of himself, just after he had shaved. It proved to be one of the most expensive self-portraits of all time, selling in 1998 for $75.1 million in New York. The painting, which the artist gave to his mother as a birthday present was, at the time it sold, the third most expensive painting ever sold.

Self-portrait Dedicated to Gauguin
(1888)

• Oil on canvas, 24.4 in x 20.5 in (62 cm x 52 cm)

Self-portrait, 1888. A self-portrait of the artist that was dedicated to his friend Paul Gauguin. From the collection of the Fogg Art Museum, Harvard University, Cambridge, MA, USA.
© 2013. Photo Art Media/Heritage Images/Scala, Florence

This rather gaunt self-portrait was dedicated to the artist's friend Paul Gauguin and completed in September 1888. Van Gogh was often compared to another Dutch artist, Rembrandt (1606-1669), for the prolific number of self-portraits he painted and their expressiveness. Along with Paul Cézanne, Van Gogh made self-portraits popular. The 30 self-portraits he created were all completed within a five-year period toward the end of his life. Most painters work on their self-portraits throughout their lifetime, so in this regard, Van Gogh was unusual. Even during this short time, the self-portraits of the artist are developmental and each time he produced a further painting of himself, it provided a fresh, new experience.

Self-portrait In Front of Easel

(1888)

- Oil on canvas, 25.6 in x 19.9 in (65 cm x 50.5 cm)

Gogh, Vincent Van (1853-1890): Portrait as a painter, 1888. Amsterdam, Van Gogh Museum. Oil on canvas, 65 x 50 cm. © 2013. DeAgostini Picture Library/Scala, Florence

This self-portrait of the artist, completed in 1888, shows Van Gogh's contrasts in typical style. While the painting almost appears like an old master in its brushstrokes, the juxtaposition of color – in the artist's jacket and paints, along with the flowing movement of these colors – contrasts starkly against the immovable figure who sits squarely in the center of the canvas with his staring eyes and set mouth. While the clever use of bold color provides exquisite interest, the subject seems to be paralyzed in time. Whether Van Gogh intended this or rather wanted to show focus and concentration is unclear.

Van Gogh

In The 21st Century

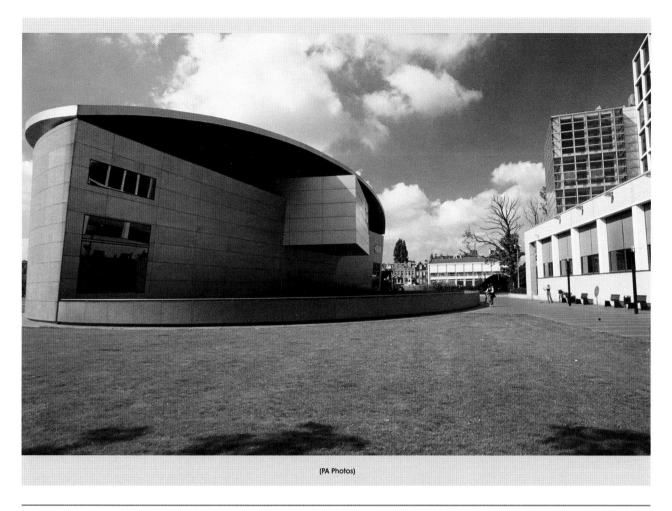

(PA Photos)

■ **ABOVE: The Van Gogh Museum, Amsterdam, the Netherlands.**

Of the total number of known works by Van Gogh, a significant number (85) of these are recorded as missing or their whereabouts unknown. It is possible that some are held in private collections, although others, undoubtedly, are permanently lost. Van Gogh destroyed some of his earlier pieces when they failed to meet expectation, but amazingly, only six works are known to have been documented as destroyed. These six paintings were all destroyed by fire – five during the Second World War. One of these includes *Still Life: Vase with Five Sunflowers,* which was part of the Sunflowers series created for Van Gogh's Studio of the South, where he had intended to set up an art school. The painting, which was in the private collection of Koyata Yamamoto, was destroyed by fire following an American air raid on Japan in 1945. *The Painter on his way to Work,* also entitled *The Painter on the Road to Tarascon* was similarly destroyed, while *Donkey Cart with Boy and Scheveningen Woman* met the same fate in 1940 in

Rotterdam, as did *The Parsonage Garden at Nuenen with Pond and Figures. The Park at Arles with the Entrance Seen through the Trees* was also destroyed during wartime, while *Windmill on Montmartre* survived until 1967.

Today, many Van Gogh's are housed in museums and galleries across the world. A large number of these works have been subject to art heists. Some have been found and returned to their rightful owners and museums, while others have never been recovered. In August 2010, some 32 years after it was first stolen, *Poppy Flowers (Vase with Viscaria)* was stolen from a museum in Cairo. Its whereabouts remain unknown. *Blossoming Chestnut Branches* was stolen in Switzerland in February 2008 but was recovered in a car some nine days later in Zurich.

Van Gogh's paintings provide links from Impressionism with their unique vision, brush strokes, and use of color, through to Abstract Expressionism. It is widely recognized that the final two to three years of his life produced his

(PA Photos)

■ **ABOVE:** The restored painting of *Vincent's Bedroom in Arles* sits on an easel at the Van Gogh Museum in Amsterdam, 2010. Van Gogh must have been horrified when he returned to his studio from hospital early in 1889 to find one of his favorite paintings damaged by moisture. He pressed newspaper to the canvas to protect it from further deterioration, rolled it up, and sent it to his brother Theo in Paris. Restorers could still see traces of newsprint when they looked at it under a microscope. They completed a painstaking six-month restoration of the masterpiece, before returning the picture to its place on the wall of the Van Gogh Museum.

■ **OPPOSITE:** Kirk Douglas portrays Vincent Van Gogh in the 1958 film, *Lust for Life*. Douglas received a best actor Oscar nomination for his role.

most acclaimed works, yet his technique, movement, and subject matter have influenced thousands of artists since his death to the present day. Abstract Expressionist artists of the New York School used his lines and distortion of reality for emotional effect as a guiding principle, while shortly following his death he became a strong influence on the next generation of artists. Fauvism, advocated by Matisse (1869-1954), was heavily influenced in color by Van Gogh, while the German Expressionists also followed his bold use of color. Later came Abstract Expressionists, including Pollock, who used sweeping, experimental brush strokes. Contemporary artists who are greatly influenced by the Dutch painter are Stefan Duncan, who has created a style he calls Squigglism, Lee Tiller, a contemporary Impressionist, Vitali Komrov, Cameron Cross, creator of The Big Easel project, and sculptor Jim Pallas.

Van Gogh is big business today in all sorts of guises from bags, aprons, umbrellas, and other merchandise, to novelty items. He remains the number one artist of choice for prints and posters, and hand-painted recreations of his works are extremely popular. Van Gogh's works are also the most fraudulently copied pieces of all time. The influence that Van Gogh has had, and still has on the art world, has seen his paintings sell for tens of millions of dollars. Some of these are the most rare and sought-after acquisitions in the industry. A far cry from the creator of these magical works who lived a life in abject poverty and who described himself as "secondary."

(PA Photos)

Further information

Books

The Real Van Gogh: The Artist and His Letters, N. Bakker, L. Jansen (2010)

The Yellow House: Van Gogh, Gauguin and Nine Turbulent Weeks in Arles, M. Gayford (2007)

Van Gogh, S. Naifeh, G. White Smith (2011)

Van Gogh's Letters, V. Van Gogh, H. Anna Suh (2010)

Van Gogh to Kandinsky: Symbolist Landscape in Europe 1880-1910, R. Thomson, R. Rapetti (2012)

Van Gogh: Up Close (National Gallery of Canada), C. Homburg (2012)

Useful websites

www.vangoghbiography.com

www.vangoghgallery.com

www.vangoghletters.org

www.vggallery.com

A selection of museums

Albertina, Vienna, Austria

Ateneum Art Museum, Helsinki, Finland

Galleria Nazionale d'Arte Moderna, Rome, Italy

Hiroshima Museum of Art, Hiroshima, Japan

Israel Museum, Jerusalem, Israel

Louvre, Paris, France

Musee des Beaux-Arts, Tournai, Belgium

Museo Thyssen-Bornemisza, Madrid, Spain

Museu de Arte de Sao Paulo, Brazil

Museum of Architecture, Moscow, Russia

Museum of Fine Arts, Boston, USA

Museum of Modern Art, New York, NY, USA

Nasionalgalleriet, Oslo, Norway Germany

Nationalgalerie SMPK, Berlin,

National Gallery, London, UK

National Gallery of Canada, Ottawa, Canada

National Gallery of Ireland, Dublin, Ireland

National Gallery of Scotland, Edinburgh, Scotland

National Gallery of Victoria, Melbourne, Australia

National Museum of Wales, Cardiff, Wales, UK

National Museum of Western Art, Tokyo, Japan

National Museum, Stockholm, Sweden

Ny Carlsberg Glyptotek, Copenhagen, Denmark

Tate Gallery, London, UK

Van Gogh Museum, Amsterdam, Netherlands

10/22-2

10/22-2